THE TALE OF THE FORMLESS TRICKSTER

TOLD THROUGH 25 POEMS

GARGEE BARUAH

To the ghosts of time

You rattle me,

You release me.

Contents

Contents

Preface

The trickster is a culmination of all opposites. It refuses to be just one thing.

It embodies the wholeness of being through the scatterings of its avatars across time and space - the solve et coagula of being - as above, so below, as within, so without, as the universe, so the soul.

This collection encompasses a string of poems and fragments I have worded out of my reflection on the experience of living in relation to things surrounding the idea of the self. It is a treatise in its thought, verse and monologue in terms of articulation. I associate the self first with the archetype of a trickster because in a world of countless definitions and structures, the identities ascribed to the self aren't and can't be fixed despite the presupposed intention. Compared to certain human existence, the trickster is an anomaly, who deliberately places itself outside of this system, out of its love for the ever-unfolding curiosity and disinterest in wanting to be bound to a codex of societal categories.

Through this myriad of experiences, I assume the role of a trickster, formless, who strives to achieve self-expression through the word. And since the word is fleeting and never fixed, it therefore demands a self that is undefined and hungry for expression. It is bound to be open to interpretation, despite the initial idea of the writer/poet, and hence, I enter - not as a witness, but as a participant of the word that is yet to birth itself.

A trickster that dreams to be a creator.

Acknowledgements

Every single residue of this impermanence nurtures gratitude in me.

I am thankful

to Bijit Sinha for his faith in me to make this anthology come to life;

to Yati Sharma for her magic in creating the cover art;

to Vasundhara Malik for being the pixie dust of joy in everyday life;

to Thomas Sharp, the poet from outer space who has been a constant source of inspiration in my mini-universe.

1. Who Am I?

Wriggling through a rush,
Ringing like an accidental hum
In the left ear of a stranger,
Spilling through a tense wire
About to snap,
Disappearing into a thin high
As adrenaline,
Missing the point,
Frozen fears through a
Pretentious roughness of spirit:
I am a sad rock.

2. Liminal Walking

Home-grown Buddha, a hermit in heels.
I didn't stop by at this station to hog on gnostic falooda -
There are wisecracks and fringe corridors at every turn;
Inside my head sits a roundtable conference of insipid idea-burn.
If this is not a walking bildungsroman,
It is probably a meat sculpture
-A Bardo jam-

3. Figglepop Galactica

Little did I assume
There were faraway homes
Outside my head
And into the sun-stars,
Eating crunchy asteroids for breakfast
And pretending a catastrophic doom,
I look at you,
Your blurry face,
Our intimate jargon,
As I float like a 70's spaceship
With colours flashing
Like jigsaw lovers.
Lock up the screen inside my
Soft pop-tart eyes.
It's clicked a picture of my boo's home planet:
TV sets, undies, utensils, and dreams
Sucked into a large bowl of crater.
How big is this massive hole
Piercing through a universe of death wish?
I lay low
Upon a Kubrickean visual verse;
My heart beats in crescendo;

Come over here.
I taste you inside my head like you are matter,
Flavourful quicksand.

4. Butterfly Girl

Now she hangs, Butterfly Girl,
Amidst a stream of people
Craning their necks,
As if she's Jesus,
Her wings - a rush of abstraction,
Now brushing against one another,
Now fluctuating like power trips,
Scaly centre and toffee-flavoured,
Pop songs from a suburban gig,
A 60's memory,
Borrowed,
Crawling into my skin,
Shying away from bodies belonging inside of me;
She's sober but her head -
Light as a dream,
Wings woven out of all the currents
On reality paradoxes
And fluttering
With glittery nebulae slow-dances.
Butterfly Girl soaring
High like a memory
Being lifted, soft erasure of

Fragment narratives,
While the spine of existence
self sustains,
The ceiling broke…
And the sound of a glassy freedom
Resounding -
"Where did she go?"
Cried out lanky Ludovico
With shattered sunglasses on.
Ludovico lost his mind that day
And has never been sad a single day
Since.
In awe of the Butterfly Girl,
He makes Butterfly tees and
Folds dreams inside them to
Give away to strangers.

5. People's Potato

A skinception coursing through the banal to alter realities,
Shaking off the earth to shower in stylised sinks and
Simmering hot to make a summer dry spell less mundane,
Seasoned with magic and spice-soaked in a Bengali fish curry
As one world splits into floating halves,
Sliced thin to dance in crisp golden skirts to tame the
Tongues of the youth and old alike,
Answering questioning mouths with a humble "I am all yours";
An unsung and existential mash-up minus ad traffic,
Lovers and tired lovers entertained to keep up with the
Leela of living well-fed with convenience.
No morals for 'The Dude' vegetable - sitting in a sad
Sack of unromanticised vendor piles uncut by the idiocy
Of a fuxked nation;
No borders to dim its brown light - the humble prince of
No-indoctrination.

~Sinful and a sass bag of avatars~

6. How to Eat Ennui

I said I like bread and the theatre of the absurd
As much as I like keeping away from catharsis.
I probably like half-catharsis
Because, hey, who are you to satisfy my curiosity?
I like talking eyes
Because I am a cat.
And I am distracted, give me your shoelace.
I like talking eyes and imagining I am holding hands with
That pair of rare talking eyes.
I love walls that sit on their own
And really don't care if I would like to know how mighty they
are (the pretence of it, I mean, I like it).
But it has to be staged with sheer method x spontaneity;
That wouldn't break out of performance
If I looked away.
I like waking up and staying in bed for half an hour more
Without rushing to make the world spin faster
While I secretly sell the moon to myself.
Sometimes I talk to myself in first person and you won't get it
because I switch to second person
And the third person is confused now - "hey, activate host
person!"

So, yeah, I like bread.
I woke up the other day
And smelt like butter, so now you know I like bread -
Just can't decide which dimensions of it yet,
But I like bread.
It's soft but tight on the edge a little
But not tight enough like a shut door -
Crumbs of complexity
Spilling over the edges but self-contained mofo,
I melt.
As banal and magical a spread! I like bread. (Just found out.)

7. Speak to Me

Speak to me like a siren song
So that I may cast my nets
To catch you by the storm.
Your windy curls and unsung chills
Barring all the other sounds that howl
Above and beyond my hearing range,
Leaping and bouncing like javelin's grace,
Piercing through the mumbles of reality
To get to my soul.
My eardrums split open
Like hungry flowers ready to bloom,
Inching closer to your closing game.
Speak to me now of spring
In sun-soaked pearly footprints
By the shore.
Speak to me no more.
Speak, for sure.

8. This Everyday Affair of Death

The wings of atomic changes drive past my hungry underbelly.
Today I devour - tomorrow I get devoured,
And the cycle comes to a close of a numeric ten,
Rising like a ritual in the dead of the night,
Voicing out howls, mocking my fears,
Until the sun comes up and chirps yellowed-hopping songs,
Slight tuning here without my noticing.
A bright redness of Muladhara ecstasy in another me,
How many deathly traps I write?
How many lives are woven into myriad fantasies?
There are no rooms to lash out at the strange paradox of being.
It's like a cat gracefully rocking the damp, sullen nightly walls for food.
Hunger is pushing me forward
Or making me resent my inevitable doom.
Stillness comes and sits on me,
We sixty-nine through eternity.
What games I pull, what meditations I disappear into
Sometimes an Akshobhya, sometimes a Vajradakini!
Constantly rotating on its own axis,

A skeleton of sculptured language,
Meanings hang like a fruit season,
Until ripened to grace,
Until ripened to be infested as worm food,
But the windy-meaty bodily metaphysic continues to live
On its own,
Othering me at times - embracing me at times,
Enlivening me at all times;
A stoicism of sorts, a sorcery of sorts,
A string of poetry that consumes it all.

9. I Abhor Routine but it Catches me when I Falter

It's either a Sunday or a Thursday
And the sun still shines on time.
The birds manage to build nests near a secret window.
Despite some angry owner's wrath that might or might not
Break its new ones' flight,
I stalled getting Chihiro, my imaginary cat.
It might play the whisker monster
From my childhood, to the birds.
The owls still hoot and mean different things
To different hearing humans -
Is it good luck or
Is it an omen?
The wars take time to share their tabloid spotlight,
The phone keeps ringing, the ads get written like destiny,
The city goes bananas over time,
The cars drive on middle-class dreams, the bars pull off escapisms over techno,
Beautiful people keep getting stranger by the day,
And this scam of fingers types away like a distant hurricane,
'Solitary' cosplaying as serenity,

A multiplicity of method.

10. I was a Fortune Teller in my Dream Last Night

If it's the darkest hour of a lonesome exit and you want to sink your teeth into it, give it bite marks, and it's your love language, okay?!
If you float endlessly, another part of you blinks like time's eye, waiting for a swift landing and crashes knee-deep, earth's belly stabbed with accumulated rage for questions within questions, become sand-mouthed poems,
If you find memories and anticipations as a set of antique collections at a museum, a stranger thing and time sucked out of you, look hard at that face while it pierces your flesh, strangulates you like a nightmare;
Tell the ghosts "You can have me but make sure you cook me hella fine, because I despise half-hearted tongues. Virtues and vice can kiss my carcass!"
If you know you're a dead-end, reach it. Bring yourself flowers. Vanity. Whatever temporarily makes you stay for you.
If all you can think about is a good night's sleep, let dreams and dirges become bedfellows because they like cuddling.

11. Moon Salad

What a terrifying thing it is to not cling to familiar places that there is a strange ripple in your heart. A growing turbulence that reaches its crescendo and drops you out of yourself. You hang. In a different but still presence. You beam, you flicker, you burn out, you remember. You submit to a quiet order that asks you to accept yourself wholly with everything you've been, before and after. You drop dead and write them mad things down bleeding, minus the performance. You see, your "inner life" is no longer shying away from your own resentments with yourself.

You, a ghost town.

You, moon salad.

Go, light a smoke. Turn grey. Become thoughtless air.

Burn all you want.

Play Hamlet and mouth a dry-fluid soliloquy. Make them think you're crazy.

12. Gnothi Seauton

Did I ever pause to understand what "Know Thyself" means in its fiercest and most uncomfortable unfolding? Did I ever think so hard and so deep into every beat of this heart-shattering resounding? I have only been touching the outer rings of a brazen flame that knows its entire existence depends on how insanely it burns. While I strive and seek to burn down every outer layer of my identity to keep reaching inwards endlessly, the growls keep growing louder, my eyes pierce through all the inner eyes still reverberating like an infinite tunnel of erotic wisps clearing the farce bubble of existence. Every dare is a death sentence. Every turn leads to gasps and horrors of finding the self. Did I think reaching far and wide into my own cavern would feel like crossing the abyss? Only thought about it in Philosophy classes, never knew it could be felt. Even yawned over it with ecstasy. There's a massive eruption of heart work cracking up the skull of a borrowed identity. It's never to be reached, but it's worth all the swims into the vortex. Did I think poetry is to be embodied and not just written? There goes a shot to my head.

13. I was once a Scheherazade

I was once a Scheherazade
Holding death at a story's length
And if death trembled to come get me,
It would bite the edges of the bed
Or chew the wooden sides of antique windows.
There was atheism in that house
But the love gurgled like prayer streams.
When rain peaked at midnight kissings,
Thunderstorms would leak through our veins.
Each time, a king died
Scheherazade couldn't write.

14. Euripedes' Medea and the East's Dark Mother : Love, Nonetheless

We choose our teachers. We choose our lovers.
My guilty pleasures open me up to my grosser parts I shut out from seeing the light of day. Since I keep my children, the principled ones and the rogues apart, they tear up the walls.
One set longing to exchange bodies with the other.
Minds ruffled up to create disco out of the panic room. Calmness hangs above as I bathe in muck, attach my sense of being with the temptations that enthrall my temporality. Once again when I levitate towards a blissful nothingness, all my children below raise their hands to grab hold of me, to feed on my warmth, to inspire my rage and love alike. My demonic children with hearts of gilded playfulness.
My wise and aloof, feathery-light wisps of a quiet ruse. My teachers come as I summon them. My lovers like poems etched in my skin. And then I become the mother of the wicked children, my skin sheds memory to wear another shield against the humdrum, another hunt beneath the sandfills of the night. This is how a breath births a hum. A hum turns into a lullaby. A kiss tongueing a hiss. My children, my skin and my heart. My past

and future crafted into amulets.

~My post-fiction, a premeditated another life~

15. For Puck's Sake

Sometimes, the sky rattles
With the fear of abandonment.
What if I get lost behind
A foggy screen of mourning?
When warm blankets turn into
Sappy Netflix romedies,
Putting love in boxes made out of
Content strategy for the fools.
Where love is akin to wondering,
Yearning - losing - dying,
Kissing the frog prince,
Or swiping right on wooden faces.
A loss of appetite for moans
That look like The New York Times Bestsellers,
But a leaning towards an unveiling
That says Death for a tarot card.
In a world of wars,
Love is a gun
Cocking for salvation.

16. Moon People

Another day is beautiful because…
The magical hop of a praying mantis reminded me
When I was six
That I was going to meet phantoms in the dark
And they'd bring me chalices
Pouring like fountains,
Ritualistic and fluid dance movements about the night
Emanating hoarse and cataclysmic moans.
My heart split into multiple forms
Taking notes on how to swallow pasts,
All springing about the greener pastures,
Clinging to hope and fiddling with river spirits,
A sorcerer with gleaming blue eyes and not the blue-bearded one
Clarissa Pinkola Estes warned me about,
Shows up.
Although another one I had chanced upon
In a full moon night earlier
left me with questions made
Of multilingual sprites - sensuous moon beams
And persistence in kissing,
A whole creation births and destroys itself
In between,

A middle realm where I float.
Him, a damned goat, antique and
Silver-plated horns;
I, a forlorn goddess
Hunting fresh blood trickling from the pages
Of a beating heart.
The blue-eyed sorcerer came and we held hands.
Then my room smelt like his scent.
His head felt like my curious songs
When I was six.
We creaked like noisy windows against the wind
And the storm.
Our blankets determined to wrap us in love
For a million lifetimes.
Then we go/went about our ways in search
Of poetry without any longing
Except for wakeful songs in the spirit of the night,
He is/was all the light.

17. I Will Hold your Hand Tomorrow

My most cherished memory is located at a future time
And I cannot wait to hold its wise hands.
How my neck longs for a truce!
How foolish a chuckle tucked away sounds.
~ What a moron, what a muse ~

18. Eye Contact

A flower wilting
And my axis tilting,
Thunderbolts in loud lilting,
Perfumed hair knots
Split like snakes
Disjointed from a curse.
Medusa hissing,
Perseus kissing.
A pointless plot reverses a conundrum,
Love is Greek to me.

19. Dancing with The Serpent Fire

The world is sea-green and
Emotions cannot take you places alone.
There are boxes the size of my shoes
And some the size of a collective ego;
I need to fit in -
Thicken myself or slice myself
Into neat and delicious paper-thin
Mouth-melting butterfly slurps;
I need to fit in to see which way
The sun dangles from the evening sky
For visitors to kiss their
Could-have-been lovers.
I walk in all directions to see if
There's some fool like me
Jumping box to box,
Questioning the manuals and
Licking the sunlight with a sunscreen-less
Burnt face and longing eyes
That trip on make-believe constellations.
This heart is a terrible place to belong

As it despises being managed by hands alien and familiar.
Dogmas and ill-fated currencies
Of a minefield that births gold out of
Tears, sweat, and hypocrisy;
This world is sea-green and poems
Grow like moss, and sea nymphs
Swim against the tide
For want of reassurances from
A seemingly indifferent cosmos
That they are still magical.
A sinking heart is taught
To give up its intuitive intelligence and
Rote-learn 'How to be a God in 10 days'.
The grandeur and reckless misery of this
World and its absurdist Bible of polarised
Sacred and profanity principles
Looks like spears laced with nectar.
Imagine the thongs I'd wear
To reclaim my demoness-goddess duality.
Subtlety is as ticklish as
A fierce water fountain in a cavern to me:
Babalon or Bhuvaneshwari,
The holographic universe never fails to amuse -
I sit still and sip my coffee,
Things happen around here: a crow dead - caught
In a barbed wire; someone got promoted and has a fascist for a boss; two people madly in love

But one of them is happily married with someone else
And god is a salesman.

20. The Monologue Ate the Actor

My bones lack structure and I fake this framework of a burial ground
At your service; dakinis of beauty and lust
Slurp on these last bits.
My blooming radiance co-exists with the corpse-like magnetism of this existence;
At once I watch the world spin like an internal aghori,
At once I am menacingly deceptive
To you all mortals; come and get me,
When the celestial star birds sweeping across the night sky, many dreams ago, showed up
Everyone ran for their lives;
I ran too as I fear their sublime incandescence;
They were there to get me too
As if it's all about me,
As if nothing is about me.
This space of liberation that lives to separate,
Still knowing separation is but another deception.
I wander dreamless in a lifeless void
But then my heart is heavy in some afternoons

With all the poems you left me
To chew on which now taste like debris.
My ash is spread all over my disembodied framework of being;
Even the caterpillar and the butterfly yell at me;
Why do I defy a sacred chronology?
A whiff of incense - to bring me back to my desk
A row of ants - to show me there is this method to the madness
I get it okay? I do get it;
But I crack up at this guerilla warfare of slow living,
I crack up at the hedonistic liberation of love and receiving,
And giving and giving.
There's so much I am told to account for
As if I built this world to satiate my own
Ego that's now a Nietzschean Vesuvius.
What, Saturn? You remind me of my mum,
So much building while breaking all the same.
How many negotiations now? I am obsessed
With cleaning the last atoms known.
I am breaking, I am building,
Cracking like failed tropes at dawn;
All my characters direct their own narrative.
I watch and I yell at them
For their self-importance and fucked up routines.
And then I sit back with a fake zenmanship.
I get it, I am a faker,
I enjoy this soup of solipsism.
What holy chaos, my grand spirit,

"You fuck me up," I say,
"I fuck you up," you say.

21. The Lifespan of a Character

The rains grow greener hopes:
Still moss, not flowers;
All the dances move with a knowing,
Like stronger currents
Or birds chasing homes across another season.
One fell swoop of a dizzying head -
Chattering, changing clothes, choosing lipstick,
Exchanging acting skills, jumping the plot,
Another sun upon the stage,
Leftover reminiscence, same song -
Another face, new pair of hands like
Scissors to cut-paste the familiarity,
Still moss, or mushrooms.
Still waters,
Green as clear soup,
Greening between anahata to the furious rasa;
Momentary 'hallelujah' acceptance in the living room,
Aggression on stage,
The clouds howling, street-side stomachs forgetting their names out of hunger,

Unsure of the human weather.
Now I come out of my character;
I step out of my face under the light.
So eat me up like a brownie,
Unwire me, find plot holes,
Or push me to the wall, scatter me as
A cautionary folk tale
Spreading out as a creeper.
~ Oh, you said flowers?~

22. Little Girls and Tall Trees

Bright stick figures and colouring outside outlines,
Sketching the caricature of life's gentle nudges and harsh blows,
she somersaults in the Assamese sunlight,
Grandma's stories (burhi aai'r xadhu) for a filling afternoon.
The heat balanced out with the breeze brushing softly against sweat beads,
"Is today the day I grow up?"
The trees, grounding like the grandparents' afternoon warmth - away from the cares of the world - away from the bittersweet opulence of growing up and galloping at the speed of the wind to calm the tornado within, wind versus wind, whichever wins - leaves things destroyed on its way.
The cost of peace here with the free gift of consistency at a great conquest and risk-taking, on the land below.
The treetop is a throne of the gods, no dirt of pettiness gets there.
Solitary little girl. Warrior and peacekeeper of her spirit. The ancient priestess' cave of bones and skulls, walls mingling divinity and delusions, mixed messages and cryptic voices, wisdom and gibberish on one copper plate of rice, pulses, fried potatoes in mustard oil, and curd.

Gut instinct: climbing atop that tall palm tree and hugging it
Is a terrific sanctuary from where stories hang and bear more devils in the design -
Ripe with the immensity of a superscript, undaunted by the mere necessity of cliffhangers.
But slowly, the knowing falls on her head like an apple of divine intervention, that cliffhangers.
This cliffhanger or the next, instead, seems like a milestone, a comfortable exercise upon reflecting. Then, the going-about-it had to seem like a battlefield than a sweet songbird path, isn't it?
For the little girl is dressed in anticipation.
Battlefields but green with hope because the tall palm tree always kept cooing and calling, and calming.
And the little girl would jump-skip and climb up again and again,
To hug its toughness of the bark, the wisdom of a long life, and its unbreakable kindness.
Its kindness even grounded on its highest places.
~ The little girl and the tall palm tree: an act with one person performing both roles. ~

23. Firefly Universe

I've noticed how city buses ply in Guwahati
With sweat-infused afternoon rides
Broken into little dreams while you
And I stare outside the window
To reveal ourselves to distant skies
Turning unsolicited honking and advice
Into a smokescreen universe.
You spoke like a timeless clock
Forever hanging outside our
Contemporary realities,
The Greenhouse Cafe at Six Mile
Still looks back at your memory
Distorted with winds and the wild
Laughters in sugar cubes falling out of
Anthill-terrace landscapes.
You show up suddenly, in a forlorn movie poster,
In anticipatory museum visits,
In between glitches and meditations,
Verses formed out of a pile of
Medical prescriptions, evening streetlights,
As the background colour of an
Advertisement I just wrote,

Or as a wistful dream monologue.

We met during an entrance exam

Some ages back

And we're still writing paperblocks

Of antagonism to a disdainful-dramatic-dope af firefly-universe.

~ To Loya,

Forevers are forever. ~

24. The Sacrificial Lamb of the Author

I have visited your solitary confinement
In dreams and realities alike,
Dousing the flame caught by your
Ancient air-conditioner while
You'd slipped into hypnosis,
Grappled by the miracles
Of a woman's body.
Once while watering the plants
At your mosaic-laden front yard,
You tried to tell the difference
Between that withered flower
And your erstwhile youthfulness;
A bee-sting reminded you
That it hurts to lose yourself
To too much thinking
But you'd counter that spring-less
Analysis the very next millisecond-ed
Moment with the importance
Of your writerly composition:
"What am I without thinking

Consciously?"
The electricity bill flying flat
Gracefully like an animated drone
Lands on your face
Dictating there's always a price to pay
For hyperbolic ambitions.
And when you chew the butt of
Your black-inked gel pen,
The notebook in front of you
Mocks your tawdry habits
And the lack of a Hemingway-like
Masculine determination.
I know you've noticed me too,
Although my face changes landscapes.
According to every beautiful woman
You find yourself in awe of
On your Instagram feed
And I, without consent, am fashioned
To absorb the quirks and authenticity
Of a "real" character.
Losing agency is not my thing,
I am so diverse that if you
Let me speak
I shall burn down and rebirth, a canon,
Toss the incredulous nature of my
Ferocity at your receding hairline,
Your cap sure maintains the dizzying

Seriousness on your charming face.
But I am seldom a thing you
Scratch with nibs and make paper balls out of.
To be stuck between a pile of
Used condoms, stale meals, and rotten fish,
Only to be collected tomorrow morning
By the crows
And freed into where I had descended from:
Formlessness.
You call it writing, sure.

25. I am an Assortment of Things

The red ghosts
In my midsummer nights.
Only you turn them
Into faeries like a
Post-modern Robin Goodfellow.
Nasty, your antics.
How do you do that?
"How do I do what?"
How do you birth
Characters and trap their souls?
I have a thing for beautiful things -
Conventionally pretty things.
How do you shift my perspective?
It's as if I have switched bodies
And become a character
Of your writing.
Losing agency is never my thing.
Yet, I am here:
Your face.
"My face what?"

Your face is blending with
The darkness around.
Should I switch on the light?
Actually, let it be.
I don't like lights as much.
"You like conventionally pretty things".
I do but I also don't.
"I won't ask you to make up your mind."
I wouldn't expect you to.
My mind is another's right now
As I am in your scribbles.
I like how you use a pencil.
It gives me the hope
Of being erased.
The words want to
Jump out of your notebook,
It seems.
It's a trap, I want them
To rather run scot-free
In a pub as part of
A soap opera.
"You do like conventionally pretty
Things".
Things. Yeah.
I love things.
I wish you were a thing too.
You'd have been easier

To love then.

"You don't believe that."

I guess.

Can you shut me up?

Bio

Gargee Baruah lives her waking life looking at things and chancing upon poetry. She works as a copywriter and nibbles on ideas playfully. She could be a cat or a house plant. *The Tale of The Formless Trickster* is her second release.

Printed by Libri Plureos GmbH in Hamburg, Germany